UNDERSTANDING SEXUAL MISCONDUCT BY CLERGY

UNDERSTANDING SEXUAL MISCONDUCT BY CLERGY

A HANDBOOK FOR MINISTERS

John Allan Loftus, S.J.

THE PASTORAL PRESS

WASHINGTON DC

© 1994, The Pastoral Press

ISBN: 1-56929-024-5

The Pastoral Press
225 Sheridan Street, N.W.
Washington, DC 20011
(202) 723-1254

The Pastoral Press is the publications division of the National Association of Pastoral Musicians, a membership organization of musicians and clergy dedicated to fostering the art of musical liturgy.

Printed in the United States of America.

For the men and women of Southdown
the true Wounded Healers
who teach us all so much

CONTENTS

PREFACE

There are few in North America who have not been touched in some fashion by the repeated accusations of sexual misconduct directed against clergy and ministers of the Gospel. Sadly, many of these accusations have turned out to be accurate. As our society and culture become even more sensitized to some of the subtle and yet equally damaging ways in which sexual exploitation and abuses of power can be detected, there will be more accusations.

The climate among ministers has grown chilled; they are feeling emotions that seem new and strange. Many are finding themselves "closing down" emotionally and interpersonally. Some will admit to becoming seriously paranoid in today's atmosphere. There is a scrutiny of their personal integrity and motivation that seems unprecedented and sometimes harsh. And it hurts.

Many ministers are particularly ill equipped to process these new feelings, and they admit not knowing where to start in addressing concerns with their parishioners. There is a "logjam" of emotion and a paucity of information available. This sad experience is becoming a brand new "crisis" in rectories, seminaries, and religious communities throughout North America.

Where to start? It is in partial answer to this question that the present book is offered. It is intended to be used primarily by ministers themselves, either alone, or preferably, in groups. The material is practical and down to earth. It is the fruit of many years of hands-on experience dealing with priests, brothers, and sisters accused of professional sexual misconduct. You will not learn everything there is to know about sexual misconduct or sexual abuse. In fact, many of the most interesting professional questions will not be touched at all. This is intended to be an introductory book; it can be supplemented by a variety of psychological or forensic treatments becoming more widely available today.

Many ministers simply do not know where to start: with their own feelings, with what seem unbelievable stories about their co-workers, colleagues, and sometimes trusted mentors, with their own incredulity. Many dioceses and religious communities have already sponsored workshops to deal with these topics. But often these workshops have become dominated by legal concerns or treatment concerns, and ministers leave still wondering where to start in themselves. I hope the following pages will help.

Many of the reflections here are the result of yet other workshops designed to be introductory and personal. I thank the Society of Jesus of New England for the initial invitation to address these concerns with superiors there. Their interest and feedback were invaluable. A series of seven workshops for many of the priests and deacons of the Boston Archdiocese provided the real testing ground and convinced me of the need for something in writing. I am grateful to the Reverend John J. McCormick, the Secretary for Ministerial Personnel in Boston, for his invitation to present the material throughout the Boston area in late 1993 and early 1994.

The audiences for whom the material was originally intended were for the most part celibate priests of the Roman Catholic Church. The handbook will have that unmistakable flavor about it. Nonetheless, other ministers from differing traditions, and married or single ministers, may find some help as well. I intend to exclude no one, but a particular focus will enhance conciseness and brevity. I will use the generic terms minister or priest throughout the book to refer to all categories of ministry in whatever church.

A final note. Because this is designed as an introductory glimpse at only some issues related to this extremely broad and complex arena of professional sexual misconduct, there are areas of extreme importance that will not be treated adequately. One area that comes immediately to mind concerns the potentially devastating consequences of such misconduct in the lives of those with whom we minister. Much has recently been written about consequences to "victims." By omitting a detailed consideration of this issue I have no intention to minimize legitimate concerns. Again, supplementary materials are clearly necessary. One glimpse at a problem does not tell the whole story. It is simply a place to start.

I am acutely aware that considerations of this topic can be depressing. In fact, I was once introduced to a group of priests at a workshop on this topic with the comment that having me present was a bit like always having your local funeral director over for afternoon tea. I have been told I specialize in "psychic autopsies" for clergy. There is some truth to that; in many areas of investigation we learn from what goes wrong. Such is the case here as well. My intention is not to depress you. But there are some sobering considerations in today's climate that ministers of the gospel ignore at their own peril.

CHAPTER 1

ASSESSING MY FEELINGS

Toward the end of 1993, as luck would have it, I was in Boston for a professional conference. A colleague and I had just presented a research paper concerning priests and sexual abuse at the Association for the Treatment of Sexual Abusers (ATSA). While I was sitting at a Legal Seafood bar in downtown Boston having a bowl of clam chowder, a CNN news bulletin broke onto the overhead screen with pictures of Cardinal Bernardin in Chicago. He had been accused of sexual misconduct by a former seminarian. Graphic and lurid details played on over and over as I sat with colleagues, all of whom were professional counsellors to either victims or perpetrators of sexual abuse. It was an extraordinary group to be sitting with for this news special.

Despite my many years of working as a psychologist with fellow priests and religious involved in sexual misconduct, my own emotions at that moment flamed out of control. I was embarrassed, angry, frightened, and relieved all at the same time. In fact, there were probably many other emotions I simply could not identify, or did not want to identify. I was convinced my colleagues were staring at me and waiting for comment.

We all stammered through some initial comments, almost like taking bets on whether one believed it was possible or not. But we were, after all, a relatively hard-nosed

1

crowd of professional psychologists and psychiatrists; we all knew, of course, it was possible. That was what made some of us feel even worse. It was possible. The same story was being repeated over and over again throughout North America; it had almost become commonplace in some areas.

This experience over a bowl of chowder put me painfully in touch with the confused and confusing feelings that so many ministers have whenever they pick up a newspaper or hear a radio report about another allegation of sexual misconduct by a minister. Feelings do not come in neat packages. They are only rarely clear and distinct, like Descartes' ideas. They are most often simply a mess of conflicting and challenging notions that leave you wondering and sometimes confused. It is hard to be a feeling being.

Let me continue to use myself as an example. That evening in Boston I said I felt embarrassed, frightened, angry, and relieved—all at the same time. It can be very helpful just to "shake" the feeling a bit just to see what's there, what's real, what's lasting, or what's going to linger beyond your bowl of chowder and ruin the night. It can be terribly important to know what you are feeling. And many ministers (not to mention just about everybody else in our society) have some difficulty in identifying—let alone "processing," to use the jargon, those feelings. Let's begin by just trying to identify and name the feeling.

I was embarrassed, embarrassed at being a priest with a cardinal of my church splashed all over television this way. I was embarrassed that as a priest I was sitting with so many colleagues who knew what I did for a living, that I had worked for many years with clergy abusers and knew how plausible this could be. I was frightened at what damage this supposed revelation could cause; the whole church had gone through enough in recent times, I told myself. It is time for a break, and then this. I was also frightened, if I am to be honest, for myself. Questions like: when is this all going to end, and whose next, came rapidly to mind. I was angry. At no one in particular and, for a moment, at just about everyone: CNN, the news media, God, the church, stupid lawyers, bright lawyers, stupid priests, bright priests, you name it. I was just angry and fed up with it all. I didn't even want the rest of my soup. I was also relieved, relieved that my presentation on sexual abuse by clergy had been aired the previous day. Whew! Missed some heavy-duty press coverage on this one! I was also relieved that I was officially on sabbatical from my usual ministry. The life of a quiet psychology professor looked better and better in that two-second emotional flash at Legal Seafood.

Feelings do not come in neat packages. But they color just about everything we think and have a direct impact on our bodies too. It is very important to gain some familiarity with them. It is imperative at the outset of any discussion of sexual misconduct by ministers—especially if you are a minister yourself.

I start with a chapter on assessing your feelings quite simply because your feelings about this topic will color and give texture to everything you read or hear in the rest of the book. Feelings have got to be the starting point for our exploration. We may not **do** anything with them, but they are there and will exact their toll whether you like it or not.

In an ideal world, education on sexual misconduct for ministers would spend a good deal of time just surfacing and processing feelings about the topic. This is what has not been done in many of the workshops thus far. Information about the issue is not enough. Emotional help is called for and support, genuine, warm, human support. No book can provide that either. But at least know that the starting point must still be your own feelings. Everything else will be sifted through them.

Let me provide some examples of feelings that many ministers are having whenever this topic arises. The list is by no means exhaustive; it is meant to be suggestive. Ideally you could just begin talking honestly with a close friend or colleague whom you trust and note together what you are feeling. Sometimes just articulating the feeling is enough to give you access to ways of handling it, if some handling is required. Remember one of the hallmarks of our psychologized generation: feelings just are. They are in themselves neither good nor bad, right nor wrong, healthy nor pathological. They just are. But as they are they exert an enormous influence on the rest of our body-mind-spirit interface.

Denial

I start with denial because it is still so prevalent among ministers and because it sometimes gets a "bad rap" among people who don't seem to realize how perfectly natural and healthy a response it can be. Denial is, however, not exactly a simple feeling; it is more of a complex psychic mechanism that just sometimes feels like a feeling. These subtleties need not detain us here.

Many ministers are still in denial about the whole sexual misconduct scenario of recent years. They honestly think-feel-believe that it is not real. Some say it's all being made-up by vindictive and religiously frustrated media types. Some keep insisting that, yes, one or two "bad apples" made some little mistakes, but there's not a real significant problem among clergy. Some others simply deny the consequences of the misconduct: sure some ministers cross boundaries on occasion, but what's the big deal? Nobody really gets hurt.

These are all illustrations of the kind of denial that is still common, unfortunately, among ministers. Sometimes there is a grain of truth that makes the denial plausible. Sometimes you can hear someone saying: "I know so-and-so, and she was abused by her minister, but it didn't do any lasting damage. What causes the real damage is all this talking about it!" The grain of truth is that this minister may, indeed, not have any idea of the damage caused. So it appears that there is none. This may or may not be the real case.

Denial also operates on two sometimes different levels. Sometimes the denial is a fairly conscious affair as

4

when the media gets blamed for creating the crisis. Other times, the dynamic of the denial is more classically unconscious. It is as if I am denying something, but have no idea that I am denying it. Not conscious that I am not conscious. This is the classic defense mechanism described before the turn of the century by Sigmund Freud and others. But remember that like all other defense mechanisms, it has its purpose. We deny in order to protect ourselves. It is not a "bad" thing to do; it just happens.

My point here is that even when denial just happens, it is important to try to get some grasp on what is being denied, what is being protected, and at what price. Denial is slowly crumbling as a major defense; the rising tide of allegations of sexual misconduct against ministers is making it simply too hard to maintain. But it remains an inviting manoeuvre for some and can be dangerous if left completely unexplored.

Embarrassment

Many ministers find this feeling becoming more and more prominent in their psychic landscape. It takes two forms: personal and communal. My personal embarrassment stems perhaps from not wanting to be compared to sexual abusers, or from not wanting to look like them (an especially troubling aspect of late for those ministers who wear a distinctive garb, like a Roman collar), or just from not wanting to have to talk about this all the time. Embarrassment has its roots in shame, and dealing with shame issues has become almost a cottage industry in North America in recent years. So-called shame-based issues include everything from alcoholism to dysfunctional families, to sexual addictions. Intense shame can indeed be a breeding ground for marked pathology; embarrassment is its herald. It is worth "shaking" my sense of embarrassment about sexual misconduct just to see what drops out.

Then there is a communal embarrassment. Many are feeling ashamed for the churches. Our people deserve better, and we know it, and the only emotional response is shame. This is awful, period! We are supposed to be leaders; we are leaders. And look. Shame on all of us—for all of us. It is a powerful emotion and is capable of leading to either crippling malaise or renewed commitment. It too needs to be "shaken" a bit and explored.

Anxiety

Anxiety is another feeling that many ministers find themselves confronting. This is often more difficult to articulate unless in the company of trusted friends. But many are feeling quite nervous (anxious) for themselves because of all the publicity. Here again, questions like, when will it all end, and whose next, appear. Only this time I am not only embarrassed about it all, I am frankly scared for myself. Many ministers realize that the standards by which we are judged have shifted dramatically in recent years. They have for many professions in our society. But today's standards make many ministers quite nervous. They realize that so-called "old cases" are being dragged-up regularly these days; they are being prosecuted in ecclesiastical, civil and criminal arenas, and people are being held accountable. Leaving aside the clear and egregious instances of sexual abuse or obvious professional misconduct, many wonder and worry what they may have done themselves. These days, someone may very easily demand accountability from us for our entire professional life in ministry. The anxiety gets generated when one realizes that by today's standards, very few of us are Snow White. Sexual harassment as a category has grown remarkably; it now includes verbal innuendo, "leering" or wandering eyes, and a whole assortment of still-growing insensitivities. Anxiety seems like a quite normal response.

Anger

One of the most common emotional responses from ministers these days is anger, often really rage. Some allow it to bubble to the surface from time to time; others are

6

getting increasingly consumed by it. Anger is one of those strange feelings. To be savored it doesn't have to have an accurate object. It doesn't matter much at whom I direct my anger; it is just there and waiting to be expressed. Ministers feel angry at themselves for choices they might have made. They feel angry at perpetrators of sexual misconduct for ruining the reputation and good name of everyone else. They feel angry at the churches themselves for what is often perceived as mishandled and half-hearted damage control attitudes. They feel angry at the media-communications people for at least occasionally seeming to make mountains out of mole hills and for initiating feeding frenzies on the steps of cathedrals. They feel angry at God for either allowing this whole mess in the first place or, worse yet, for creating it to chastise the ministry. They feel angry at themselves for feeling angry.

Pity

Some ministers feel a complex mix of emotions that sometimes looks like arrogance and sometimes pity. "Pity those poor bastards who got caught" is sometimes heard shaking around in the head. Other times, it's a more arrogant motif that comes to the fore: "We really are above all this, you know. This too shall pass. All these people who think they are getting hurt! We're the only ones who have ever helped them. They will realize that again soon. It will all go away soon. Just a tempest in a tea-pot." Pity those poor folks who get so enmeshed in all this nasty stuff! This so-called pity begins to shift into our next category.

Detachment

The feeling of detachment comes close to the arrogance referred to earlier. Often, however, among certain ministers this takes the form of intellectualized "airiness." These are the "philosophical" types who would really rather debate the propriety of this entire discussion. Their comments are often replete with "shoulds" and "shouldn'ts." They try to exist somehow above all the mess secure in their educated convictions that it "shouldn't be happening." It is all the fault of society's crumbling standards, or the sad subjectivism of the times, or anti-Catholic bias. A desire to remain detached is understandable, but it is quite dangerous as well. Listen carefully to every "B-S" conversation shared over a few beers in the rectory, community, or seminary and you will find the detached and philosophical type well represented. It usually simply covers fears that are very private and very primal and potentially very problematic.

The list of feelings could go on and on. Take some time for yourself and ask what you are feeling. Try to capture what you felt the last time you heard of another allegation against a brother priest. Remember what it was like when you first heard a friend of yours had been accused. Feelings are among the most ephemeral aspects of personality; they shift and dart about with remarkable ease. They also never wander far from the bulls-eye of your heart.

Regardless of our feelings, however, the sexual misconduct issue for clergy and religious is serious, extensive, and will not go away. It will continue to be a major issue for many years to come. We have probably just begun to deal with it. If you are the cynical type who expects it will all blow over, try confronting one of the more pragmatic types who have been paying out millions of dollars over the past few years. Without trying to sound insensitive to the human loss and suffering in all this, should you still be wondering if this is a serious issue, think pure finances. Already many dioceses and religious communities have seen their financial resources shrink dramatically just trying to stay abreast of requests for initial appropriate assistance to victims. Many important apostolates may be adversely affected for years to come.

Regardless of what you personally feel in this regard, this is a issue of enormous significance for all church bodies and all society. It will not simply go away. What do you feel about it all?

CHAPTER 2

WHAT IS SEXUAL MISCONDUCT?

One might think of this as the easiest and simplest question to answer at the beginning. One would be dead wrong.

Part of the difficulty in addressing various questions in regard to professional sexual misconduct is the shifting terrain of the discussion. I will not even try to present a detailed map of the landscape at this point. It is simply too fluid and flexible at the moment. Whatever is said in this chapter may have to be revised before it is printed. So I will paint with broad strokes and leave the footnotes to others.

My design is to get you, as a minister, to begin to appreciate the complexity of professional responsibility in our times. If you come away more anxious or confused, you are probably on the right track. I think here of one of the participants at a workshop on this material who said he thought I should not emphasize the confusion regarding definitions of sexual misconduct quite so much. He felt it was just "upsetting the men." I apologize here as I did there. But I do feel that I would rather you, the reader, to be confused and uncertain now and with me, rather than later and with your attorney.

With Minors

There are some things that can be said with relative clarity and finality. Any explicitly sexual contact with a minor (an under-aged person usually up to age sixteen legally) is clearly and definitively sexual misconduct. There is little discussion warranted here. As I am fond of saying at workshops, if you think there are still mitigating circumstances with minors, or that this is still a grey area that merits further discussion, please see me afterwards for a business card. You need help. Anyone who is going to have physical contact of a sexual nature with a minor, boy or girl, blood-relative or not, friend or foe, "professional" prostitute or "lover," will be held responsible, most likely, for perpetrating acts of sexual abuse. Don't be stupid. **There are no mitigating circumstances,** period! If you have ever had desires for such contact, or still even on occasion think about such contacts with minors, talk to someone now. The stakes for everyone are too high.

Having said this much, welcome to the grey zone. Just to stay with minors for a moment, what about not-obviously-sexual contact? What about sexual innuendo? What is a sexual overture? Who determines any of the above?

There is no clear line here; nor is there a clear code of ethics—yet. Increasingly, however, gestures, comments, even eyebrow movement can be seen as sexually disruptive—and occasionally assaultive—behavior. Language itself can be judged to be "abusive" in the heaviest sense of that word abuse. **Times have irrevocably changed.**

Who determines what is or is not a sexual overture? The "victim." If a comment or gesture is considered to be sexually inappropriate by someone, it is usually said to be so by police and courts these days. Some may want to decry this as a sad subjectivism rampant in our culture, but don't miss the main point here. It is the reality of our moment in history. You ignore it at your peril. You will not be judged on the basis of what you intended to do or say; you will be judged on the basis of what was "heard." This

10

is not as strange as it might first appear. In all my years of dealing with clergy and religious involved in some kind of sexual misconduct, I have never met one who **intended** to hurt anyone. This is precisely the point. Most "perpetrators" of sexual misconduct actually think they are being helpful or loving or, at worst, humorous. Ministers rarely intend to hurt anyone; this does not mean they do not.

It is no longer enough (if indeed it ever was) to just "trust your instincts" and "do what seems right" in a situation with young people. You must re-educate yourself to see or hear yourself from the others' point of view. Could my gesture or comment be misconstrued? What might this look like to a passerby, to a wandering police cruiser, to a court officer? We will discuss paranoia in a little bit, but the main point here cannot be overlooked: if a gesture or comment is deemed by another to be sexually suggestive or inappropriate, it will be seen so by the guardians of our culture. At some point down the line some balance may return in what is becoming for many an almost intolerable presumption of guilt. For the present, being forewarned is forearmed.

But inappropriate comments or gestures with minors (legally under-age persons) are not the most serious challenge ministers face. Age-inappropriate sexual contact represents only a small fraction of the complaints being received by authorities these days. The far larger problem revolves around sexual comments or gestures with age-appropriate persons, young adults and adults. **The sexual abuse of minors is only the tip of the iceberg.**

The media and others were appropriately enough outraged at the initial reports of child sexual abuse being reported as perpetrated by ministers. For months (perhaps years), this provided the focus for the anger and shock so many felt. But as horrific as it all seemed, everyone sober seemed to realize that there were not that many cases of clear pedophilia around. Even one was bad enough, most realized, but were there really **that many**? No, not really. Early "guesstimates" by people like A.W. Richard Sipe

(1990) put the figure at about 3-5 percent of the Roman Catholic priests. Other more careful research studies essentially corroborated the early guesses; one large-scale survey of over thirteen hundred priests and brothers over a twenty-five year period came up with a figure of 2.7 percent (Loftus & Camargo, 1994). These are not statistically large numbers and seem to be about the same as one might expect in any other large, professional sample of teachers, or doctors, or psychologists. But while some church authorities wanted to take comfort in the small numbers, the other shoe was about to drop.

With Older People

At least among Roman Catholic ministers, far many more cases of inappropriate sexual contact with older people were being reported. Sometimes these targets were older teen-agers, often enough they were adult parishioners or co-workers. The first group, those involved with post-pubertal adolescents are often referred to in the professional literature as **ephebophiles.**

[*Ephebos* is the Greek word meaning youth; it is to be distinguished from the other Greek word *pedos*, meaning child. Hence pedophilia refers to a predominant or exclusive attraction to **pre**-pubescent boys or girls, and ephebophilia refers to similar attractions to **post**-pubertal ones.] It seems, in fact, that the largest number of reported cases of sexual misconduct involving Roman Catholic ministers in recent years were cases of ephebophila (St. Luke Institute study, 1993; Loftus & Camargo, 1994).

At the present time, however, far many more cases of alleged professional sexual misconduct are being brought forward by adults and not by teen-agers at all. In my judgment, this represents the serious challenge for the immediate future. Ministers are being seen as violating professional boundaries in sexual ways with just about everybody. The scenario is much the same for medical doctors, psychologists and social workers, teachers, members of Congress and Parliaments, and just about everyone else in

12

positions of authority in our society. Indeed, one hears much these days of so-called "Zero-Tolerance" policies being implemented at all levels and throughout all sectors of our professional worlds. Clergy and ministers are no exception. The critical need for input from ministers to these fast-growing and shiny-new "codes of ethics" will be dealt with later.

The Minister's Unique Burden

Although no profession is immune to this new sensitivity and demand for increasing accountability, ministers carry a unique burden. Much of the anger and rage and hurt in cases of professional sexual misconduct is magnified when the offender is a minister. This is not a new observation and there are many obvious reasons: the "higher" standard to which ministers hold themselves, the specialness of that religiously-sanctioned relationship, the analog to family bonds that a minister and parishioner enjoy. But one other factor not to be overlooked concerns the fact that it is the minister, most often, who has for many years (centuries for some) designed and maintained the code of sexual ethics for society. Ministers have always had a special place in their hearts and sermons for the "sins of the flesh." It seems to be coming back to haunt some of them now, and those in the pews are outraged, understandably so.

In some traditions the problem is even worse. Roman Catholics, for example, often saw Father as the guardian of the bedroom; he pronounced on what could and could not be done, and by whom, and when, and how—often in meticulous detail. It was an often painful and exacting sexual ethic that was rather relentlessly drummed-in to adolescent and adult heads and hearts. It was clear in its denunciation of all sexual gratification outside of heterosexual, monogamous and life-long marriage. And now look. Father seems to have been "getting it" himself on the side all these years! No wonder some of the anger and hurt seems out of control sometimes.

13

The fact that self-professed celibates have any sexual life of which to speak causes lots of anger to surface. We trained our people well in the "old days." Some actually seem to have believed that priests and sisters "gave up" all sexuality with their vows. And now there are some Catholics, and others, who are secretly delighted at the hypocrisy being exposed among those who have for so long dictated sexual mores to them. Do not underestimate the feelings or the level of feelings that run around these issues.

What Constitutes Sexual Misconduct?

With all this as chilling background, we return to the original question: what exactly constitutes professional sexual misconduct? Let me summarize one of the most succinct explorations of this topic provided by a professional who has worked often with medical doctors and their guidelines and codes of ethics. Richard Irons, M.D. (1991) suggests that professional sexual misconduct can be defined as any overt or covert expression by a professional toward another, with whom one has a professional relationship, of any erotic or romantic thoughts, feelings or gestures that are sexual, or may be reasonably construed by the other to be sexual. Further, sexual offense is constituted by any non-diagnostic or non-therapeutic attempt to make any contact with, or touch, any anatomic area of another's body commonly considered to be sexual or reproductive. Areas of conduct include verbal sexual innuendos, other verbal or physical improprieties (such as non-therapeutic hugs), or any erotically charged encounter with the other whether inside or outside of the office. Irons concludes that this is highly charged emotional, legal, and moral terrain and that it is an area that is quite irregular and filled with many ambiguities and grey zones.

Listen carefully to the direction in which this code of ethics is moving. It is very broad, indeed. Any romantic or erotic thoughts, feelings, gestures that are either overt **or covert.** What is a covert, romantic feeling? How does one distinguish a non-therapeutic hug from a therapeutic one?

14

How exactly does one define an erotically-charged encounter? There could be some simple, clear scenarios on which we would all agree. Then there will be the grey areas. Indeed.

Professional Standards

Many of the new codes of professional ethics are being designed by members of the professions themselves. Hence psychologists determine what constitutes professional standards for psychologists, physicians for physicians, and lawyers for lawyers. As ministers we have a long road ahead of us. Many of us are still aghast that there should be such a need for commonly recognized standards. But there clearly is. And in the absence of proactive stances by ministers, legislatures and courts impose what they deem reasonable. This process will continue, with or without actual input from ministers, for the next few years. We will have to live with the consequences.

In some jurisdictions legislative law has already been enacted setting up professional standards for clergy and ministers. Many more will follow. One of the more thorny questions to arise in this legislation concerns how to define just what constitutes a "professional" relationship between a minister and another. Does the person have to be a parishioner? A card-carrying parishioner? A member of the same faith? Can it be an acquaintance who just pops in for a question or two? The questions go on. The answers have real consequences.

Most ministers are not holed-up all day in offices; they do not exercise their professional responsibilities from 9 to 5, or in any single location. Would that it were as simple as that. Most ministers have very fluid lines between the "professional" and the personal, and the lives of their charges intertwine with their own day-in and day-out.

One pointed example might clarify the dilemma. Psychologists are officially discouraged from social contacts with their clients or patients. Nor are they to enter into what are called "dual relationships," ones in which roles

15

are confused or ones in which barter becomes the means of payment for services rendered. All these kinds of relationships are seen as violating the professional code of ethics for psychologists. How many ministers have the luxury of such clear boundaries? Very few, I suspect. Pastors routinely dine with parishioners, go to shows with them, swap services with plumbers and electricians, and generally try to maintain as close and familiar a relationship as possible. This is often particularly true with the youngsters in the parish. The code of professional ethics for ministers needs realistic input from ministers. Otherwise some pretty strange codes may be enacted.

One jurisdiction in the United States now speaks of clergy sexual misconduct occurring whenever there has been any unwanted gesture or comment of a sexual nature between a minister and anyone for whom that minister has had pastoral solicitude. One wag commented that one should be very careful talking to strangers on airplanes in the airspace over this jurisdiction; a farewell hug could land you in jail—assuming you had some pastoral solicitude for your companion. This is a very broad definition, to be sure.

What is important to realize here is that the standard now used in almost all cases of misconduct concerns **inequity in power** in relationships. Here is the nub—and it disturbs many ministers. Our society clearly defines ministers as powerful persons. Very powerful, indeed. Many ministers themselves have a hard time thinking of themselves as powerful. Often their self-image is quite the opposite, and even more often they would be hard pressed to think of themselves as powerful having just returned from a parish council meeting or staff gathering at which everyone else's opinion held sway. But in the eyes of our society and culture we are powerful men and women. All our professional relationships are, therefore, by definition, inequitous. All of them! Again, whether you **feel** powerful or not is quite irrelevant. As a minister, you are always involved with what will be seen as an inequitous relationship.

It should be clear that standards are changing and have already changed significantly. As I mentioned earlier, times have irrevocably changed. But to make matters even worse, present standards are being widely used to judge past behavior. Professionals of all stripes are finding themselves held to account for actions from many years ago based on today's understandings. Again, you may want to lament or protest, or whatever; do not miss the point however. This is today's reality.

Several jurisdictions in the United States are either in the process of changing, or have already changed, their statue-of-limitations laws to allow the prosecution of any and all previous activities deemed illegal. Sexual misconduct from many years ago can now be prosecuted provided only that the victim's memories of the events were "repressed" until recently, or they did not realize the behavior was assaultive or abusive until a later time. In some cases, laws have been changed to allow for prosecution later if a perpetrator has left that jurisdiction for a time. In other words, the clock only ticks while the perpetrator is in the State or Province. This was the case in the now infamous James Porter trial in Massachusetts.

The entire sphere of so-called "repressed" memories of abuse is not without its critics. *Time* magazine (Nov. 19, 1993) ran an unusually thoughtful piece on the controversy surrounding such repressed memories. The professionals will continue their debate. But in the meantime, such "repressed" memories still offer powerful testament in courts and in the press.

Ministers need to be increasingly aware that our lives are under scrutiny in a wholly new way—particularly our personal and affective lives. Not since the sixteenth century, perhaps, has there been quite so much interest and concern about ministers' personal lives. You can take some consolation from the fact that this is not the first time in the

17

church's history that the private lives of the clerics have been questioned. William Manchester (1993) paints a picture of an earlier period that makes own look positively tame. It might hearten you to read it for some perspective. Nonetheless, we live in a time when even **the appearance of impropriety** must be avoided. It is not easy to know exactly what constitutes professional sexual misconduct, but you can be assured that the benefit of the doubt will not be yours in today's climate.

CHAPTER 3

SOME EXAMPLES

One of the easiest ways to learn about the terrain of sexual misconduct is to learn from the mistakes of others. Again and again the case study method has proven the most useful and most direct in allowing ministers to begin to get a deeper feel for the present dangers associated with this issue.

There is no doubt that some ministers are afflicted with a specific and debilitating psychosexual dysfunction that occasions their sexual indiscretions. These men need the best professional help available and we all need to realize that these disorders occasion life-long struggles; many of these disorders represent permanent aberrations in one's psychic and psychosexual makeup. The behavior occasioned by these disorders will not simply go away, nor will all the "good will" in the world, or firm purposes of amendment, make it all better.

But there are other ministers who can learn from the experience of these and other sad colleagues how to avoid situations and persons that place them in danger as well. At various workshops that have presented case examples, more than one minister has been heard leaving muttering: "There but for the grace of God go I." Most sexual offenders in ministry are not deranged monsters who appear suddenly as if from nowhere. This whole book is based on the premise that we can learn from each others' mistakes.

Broad, composite scenarios will be presented for your own consideration. Each illustration represents either a real case example or a composite of several similar cases. All have been disguised carefully to avoid any betrayal of confidences except in cases where public records are already widely available. In my judgment, these examples cover the broad range of behaviors for which ministers have been arrested, indicted, or accused in church proceedings. They will also highlight the tremendous costs involved for all parties in such allegations. You will note, no doubt, that there are no simple stereotypes here among the accused. This is the reality of today's church.

The cases will be offered without much additional commentary. My hope here is not so much to dissect or even analyze each experience, but to provide an overview of the kinds of experiences that are now commonly considered professional sexual misconduct.

1. The Pizza Party Pastor

This is the story of a middle age pastor of a large suburban parish. He was deeply loved by most of the people in the parish, known as a fairly conservative man both theologically and personally, and, in most respects, a model priest. He even had associates, fellow priests, who actually respected and liked him; the parish staff was also content and energized.

The parish had a long-standing tradition of throwing a pizza party for all those who helped with liturgies at special times of the year. The rectory was thrown open and all were welcome, including the altar servers and young people who did various jobs throughout Holy Week. This tradition had been going on for years; no one ever gave it a second thought that sometimes some of the young people would stay overnight after the party. They did on other occasions as well. Then came this year. The morning after

20

the party, one of the young men, an altar server, told his parents that during the night the pastor had fondled him.

Three young men had stayed overnight at the rectory. To this day, two swear that they neither saw nor heard anything unusual. They were all staying in the pastor's suite. They had all stayed there before this night as well, without incident. These two young men still swear to uphold the good name of the pastor. Not so the third. He still claims that after some initial chat had died down, the pastor came across the room to the small sofa bed on which he was sleeping alone, and quietly got in the bed with him. A little uncomfortable, but not terribly alarmed, the young man turned over. He claims the pastor then put his arm around him and began rubbing his shoulders. Next a hand went down to his crotch and felt him through the bed clothes. At this point he remembers saying "no, please don't," and the pastor left the bed.

The pastor was confronted early the next morning by angry parents with threats of police action. The parents also contacted the parents of the other boys who stayed over, and then began phoning other families seeking collaboration and corroborating evidence from other occasions. The pastor, meanwhile, continued to deny that he had ever left his bed—on this or any other occasion. He vehemently denied any wrongdoing and started to phone parishioners himself with tales of what was going on.

Within a few hours, higher church authorities had been notified as well as the police. The latter initiated an investigation almost immediately, and church authorities followed within a day or two. The investigation of this reported incident transpired over the next six months; it was complete with depositions from various parishioners and thorough background checks on the pastor by both civil and ecclesiastical tribunals. The financial outlay on both sides came close to a half-million dollars—just in the investigative stage. In the end, no legal charges were ever laid. There was simply no corroborating evidence, and there were two

21

eye witnesses who claimed nothing had ever happened. There was nothing in the pastor's background to support suspicions of any previous transgressions—at least not at this stage of the investigation.

To this day there is no clear or compelling evidence as to what might actually have happened. The pastor, however, has been removed from the parish. He was recommended for psychiatric care because of the incident and its aftermath, and it is questionable that he will ever again be allowed to serve as pastor in this area. The allegation itself had become so public that "scandal to the faithful" could not be avoided.

2. The Wealthy Prostitute

This story involves a minister in his early 40s, ripe for mid-life crisis. Indeed, part of his crisis was devoted to finally coming to grips with his own sexuality. As a celibate minister he had long wondered about his sexual orientation. Am I gay or straight? In his desire to find a more secure answer, he chose to "get some experience." Figuring he was probably predominantly homosexual based on his feelings and fantasies, he made his first few drives past the gay cruising area of the next town. Eventually mustering the courage, he picked-up a hustler and paid for some quick sex in the car. This was repeated on several other occasions with the same person. They both enjoyed the sex, and after a while the young hustler stopped asking for money and just enjoyed being with the minister. They became friends.

The friendship blossomed into a more or less permanent relationship for both of them. In reality, they became lovers. The young man would spend much of his time at the minister's home; they slept together regularly, and it looked like it might last forevermore. The relationship did last almost seven years, but then collapsed dramatically.

The young man, now in his early twenties, told the minister he wanted to end their relationship. He was moving away and needed some money. He told the minister that if he did not provide a large sum of money, he would go to the minister's religious superiors and charge him with child abuse. It seems the young man had been only sixteen years old when they first met. The young man assured the minister that legally it would not matter much that he had been a "professional" at the time.

The minister beat the young man to the punch, confessing the entire affair to his superiors. In order to avoid the scandal and potential embarrassment to the minister and his colleagues, they agreed to settle out of court for 1.2 million dollars.

3. The Ancient Missionary Tale

This is the story of an older man—in his late seventies when we first had contact—who had spent his entire life ministering in a foreign land. When first assigned to this territory, a much younger missionary, filled with zeal and enthusiasm, found himself getting "caught" sampling the local culture a bit too thoroughly. He got involved sexually with one of the young women of the area and they spent one night together. This was the only time they were together, and this was, apparently, the only one with whom he ever got involved sexually.

The minister realized quickly the violations involved here: of the young woman, of his commitment to the mission, and of his own public commitment as a priest. He went immediately to his local superior and "confessed" his transgression. Both he and the superior spoke with the young woman and offered apologies as well as assistance. It was a swift and relatively thorough response, perhaps unusually so considering this incident took place over twenty-five years ago and in a foreign country.

All parties felt comfortable that this was the end of the story. Nothing was heard about it or said about it for decades. Until quite recently.

A much younger priest was recently missioned to this same territory. He came to his ministry armed with a much more contemporary social science background, and with images of recent sexual misconduct scandals throughout North America fresh in his mind. He was talking about the sexual "scene" in North America with one of the older woman in the area when she rather calmly said that it certainly did not occur only in North America. In fact, she went on to say, she herself had been a victim of just such misconduct many years earlier and right here in her own backyard. As the fates would have it, this young priest had found himself in conversation with the woman who had been abused by the older priest some twenty-five years ago.

The younger priest turned to his superior aghast that this incident had not been dealt with more publicly and said that he was going to take it upon himself to find out if there were any other instances of sexual misconduct by his colleagues at the mission. This he proceeded to do—some might even say with a vengeance, or at least with an enthusiasm that seemed unparalleled in this tiny community. The net result has been a turmoil within the community that has almost torn it apart.

There are now rumors and vague accusations flowing all about. Generations of missionaries are held in suspicion and investigations continue to this day. Church authorities felt they had no choice but to respond with thoroughness and conviction to all allegations. There are hundreds of ongoing investigations with little hope of any coming to satisfactory conclusions, according to many on the local scene. Too many natives of the area either do not remember, or do not want to remember, anything; others are scandalized even at the suggestion that these "good Fathers" should be accused this way, and in many cases twenty-five or thirty years has passed. Many of the stories are told about people, both alleged perpetrators and victims, who are now dead. Reputations on all sides are seriously compromised.

The toll in both emotional and financial terms has been staggering. One person in a leadership position today suggests that the mission will simply never recover any semblance of healthy functioning again. Religious authorities have already drafted contingency plans for closing down their involvement and leaving the area. Obviously this cannot be contemplated seriously until all are satisfied that investigations have been completed. It will be a long road and the costs to all are heavy indeed.

4. The Hundred Victim Predator

These are the kind of stories that grab headlines. I will tell the story of only one of the priests who appears to have systematically and callously preyed upon many young people over many years. Despite the "headline" quality to all these cases, they do not represent the greatest threat or challenge in understanding professional sexual misconduct. They are simply too obvious and blatant. As suggested earlier, whereas this type of incident does happen, it by no means represents the largest part of the problem with ministers and sexual misconduct; it is, nonetheless, chilling in the re-telling.

This is the story of a much beloved priest who had dedicated his entire life to working with Native peoples. He was so successful that upon his death a formal request was made by the Band Council to the religious authorities. The native community wanted this priest to be allowed to be buried in their sacred burial grounds with full Native honors. The request was readily honored and the priest's family as well as his colleagues enjoyed the ceremony greatly. For the moment, all seemed tranquil.

Shortly after his death, however, rumors began circulating throughout the community that perhaps they had desecrated their sacred grounds by this gesture. Initially only one or two young men began to talk of sexual abuse at Father's hands. But it was enough to set a dis-ease in motion that saps energies to this day. Gradually and quite quietly several more young men spoke of their own abuse. Word got back to the religious authorities and they initiated a quiet investigation themselves. The results of that initial quiet investigation have reverberated for several years and the consequences to just about everyone in this Native community have been dire.

To make a very long and painful story short, more thorough investigations have revealed that there are at least forty primary victims of this priest's sexual misconduct. There may be many more. The consequences for secondary and even tertiary victims is exacerbated by the peculiar communal sensitivities in a native community. To borrow a quaint phrase, all hell broke out. At times it seemed so quite literally.

A deeply sensitive and massive campaign was mounted by the religious authorities in this case to uncover all misconduct by this priest or any others serving this community. Financial assistance was provided almost immediately to primary victims; psychological services were provided both on and off the reserve. A joint committee was established to attempt a "Reconciliation Model" for future assistance and to determine what compensation could be offered not only to individuals involved, but to the entire community.

As this is written, there is yet no closure in this situation. There may not be for many more years. But already, millions of dollars have been spent and hundreds of lives permanently altered by the process itself. It has been devastating for all concerned—and is not over yet. Meanwhile, other aspects of the investigation continue. Other priests and brothers missioned to this reserve are being questioned; other potential victims are being interviewed; other geographical sites are being explored for possible abuse there. In the end, there may turn out to have been hundreds of victims over a period of many years.

A final aside on this illustration, the atmosphere in which these investigations continues is growing more hostile as time unfolds. One of the major reasons concerns the long history of White culture's dominance over Native peoples. There is need for very careful articulation on both sides here. Explicit sexual abuse is viewed by many as only one further illustration of a more general abusive pattern repeated again and again throughout North America by White, European missionaries. It is a highly charged atmosphere for all involved.

5. The Loneliness of Father-Uncle

This example involves a terribly respected and well-liked, fifty-five year old priest who simply accepted a family's invitation to take a holiday with them. It was even his own family. His sister, her husband, and two children invited Father to join them for an ocean cruise. It was a delightful experience for all until several days out. All the calculated romance of the cruise was not wasted on the minister; he found himself getting more and more frustrated and angry and lonely watching couples having such a grand time together.

Late on the third night, his sixteen year old nephew joined him for a "nightcap" in one of the lounges. Even a sixteen year old can imbibe a bit in international waters. Afterwards, both the priest and his nephew went back to a cabin, the minister's cabin. There Father began talking about his life and loneliness, as he continued to drink. Finally, he put his arm around his nephew, "cuddled" him, and dragged him playfully into his bed. The minister made a fumbling attempt to grab his nephew's rear-end before the nephew jumped up and ran out the door.

The nephew was terrified, told no one about the incident, and tried to sleep back in his parents' cabin. He was still quite shaken early the next morning and knew his mother was going to ask about it. He blurted out what had happened.

His mother was enraged and horrified. She fairly shouted to her husband what had transpired and decided there and then to confront her brother immediately. While still terribly upset, she had just left her cabin door when she ran into an officer on the ship with whom they had been friendly earlier in the cruise. When he asked if everything was alright, she stammered that it was not, and told the story of what had happened. The ship's officer calmed her down and returned her to her cabin saying he would go to see the uncle. He did go, but not until after he reported the incident to the ship's captain who insisted on accompanying him to the priest's room. When they arrived, the priest

27

was promptly "arrested" for indecent behavior on the high seas and taken into custody.

This turn of events was not what the mother had wanted. She wanted to vent her anger and then insist her brother get some help for his problem. But the entire incident had just slipped out of their control. The priest was arraigned later that week for criminal acts in international waters. His "slip," which is what he swears it was, cost him more than just his freedom. Even though there appears to be no credible evidence that any such incident had occurred before or with anyone else, he is awaiting sentencing as a sexual offender and has been dismissed from all duties in his home area.

6. The Meandering University Professor

An extremely well-known and respected professor was reported to university officials for sexual harassment and/or assault. It seems that initially one of his graduate students, a young man, had grown so uncomfortable with this professor's "attitude" and "sexually charged" style that he spoke to a faculty advisor about it. The advisor dismissed the complaint in the beginning saying that this professor "always shows some affection to his students . . . it's just his way."

When this student had the opportunity to talk with another graduate student of this same professor, he heard a tale that sounded remarkably familiar. They talked to yet others. No one ever had been the object of explicitly sexual overtures, but all had experienced the same discomfort, and all named it, at least generally, sexual.

Bolstered by their communal experiences, two of the students approached university officials with their observations. The officials promised to look into the matter. Indeed, they did bring these new observations to an older and wizened priest on campus. His response was simply: "Oh no, not again!" It seems that at least a vague discomfort had been expressed by students as far back as fifteen years ago. No one ever alleged sexual abuse or direct sexual misconduct; all did say, however, that they were extremely uncomfortable in this professor's presence and especially in his rooms. Something strange had been going on for years. But the professor was also one of the most beloved preachers and ministers on campus, so nothing was ever said or done directly.

This case illustrates well how times have changed. It no longer takes an explicitly genital invasion to bring down charges of sexual misconduct. Most in our society now recognize that some of the more subtle ways of abusing power and/or sexual superiority are just as damaging and devastating. One instance might not make a "federal case," but often enough where there's smoke, there's fire; when people talk to each other, cases are built and careers come tumbling down.

This priest was eventually confronted and denied any explicitly sexual intent on his part. There were not clear enough grounds for any criminal or even civil litigation. Nonetheless, the priest was removed from his teaching position by religious superiors and more formal complaints were registered within the university. Monetary settlements were offered and accepted.

This is as good a time as any to point out that this priest (and many others like him) may not be simply lying or dissimulating about his intentions. He may, in fact, be unaware of any explicitly sexual content to his advances. A good number of ministers, unfortunately, are sincerely so out of touch with their own bodies and sexuality that they remain consciously oblivious to any sexual content in their actions or comments. But they are sincere. That makes it even more dangerous.

Sexual repression has long been a hallmark of seminary training in some traditions. Along with so-called sublimation and conscious suppression of unwanted sexual urges, repression has long been cultivated as an attractive methodology for dealing with sexuality. It is by no means restricted to ministerial formation either. Just think of how often in response to one of your own questions about sexual issues, you might have heard some well-intentioned person say: "It's all right. What you don't know can't hurt you." Nothing could be further from the truth.

7. The Hugging Spiritual Director

This illustration will continue themes developed in the previous example. Here we have an older gentleman who had been involved with spiritual direction for years and years. He was, again, extremely well known and respected and a much sought-after guide in many circles. This priest received mandated psychiatric care for repeated instances of hugging in what were perceived as clearly "non-therapeutic" ways.

As in the previous example, we have here an illustration of what many have come to call today, "boundary" violations. Again, there were never any allegations of explicitly sexual (genital) indiscretions. But this spiritual guide always took a detailed sexual history from those with whom he was working, and always spent a great deal of time and energy discussing their sexual histories and experiences. His "hugging," which had been a consistent part of his spiritual direction style for many years, was the final straw for some. At first, it didn't seem out of the ordinary to always hug at the end of a session. But then the "hugs" began to take on a more lingering quality. After discussing sexuality for an hour, one of these lingering hugs is precisely what brought a religious woman to another priest friend for a reality check. Again, it was easily confirmed that she was not the only one who felt uncomfortable. Several had even asked the spiritual director to stop giving the hugs. All was to no avail.

This sister took her concerns higher up the ladder. When religious authorities were informed at the diocesan level, they moved swiftly to shut down the spiritual director's ministry. It appears again that many had known

30

about some "irregularities" for years, but no one broke the silence until now. As noted, the priest received some treatment and was forbidden to exercise any unsupervised ministry from that point on. To the end, however, the spiritual director remained in firm denial that he had ever done or said anything that he felt was inappropriately sexual. He blamed it all on the "crazy society" that is evolving out the sexual revolution of decades ago. He remains unrepentant and somewhat arrogant about it all.

8. The Repentant Pedophile

This case illustrates the persistence and immutability of some psychosexual disorders. It also illustrates the need for constant vigilance and careful diagnosis when dealing with psychosexual dysfunctions. The story is that of a man in his late sixties finally trying to pick up pieces of shattered lives throughout his lifetime—not the least of which are the pieces of his own tragic life.

The story begins with the parents of a former student who, after months of agonizing debate among themselves, finally phoned to ask for an interview with a religious authority. When they arrived, they calmly told a story of their son and of his suicide two years earlier. They said, further, that they had become convinced that the suicide was precipitated by several acts of sexual abuse that had taken place several years ago at the hands of one of their son's high school teachers, a priest. They only wanted to ensure that no others had been victimized by this man, and that he receive some help for his problem.

Without going into all the details, suffice it to say, that upon investigation, the religious authorities came to believe that the parents' association of their son's suicide with sexual misconduct by one of their priests was well founded. The priest was questioned and immediately admitted the abusive relationship; he described in great detail and with great remorse just how it all evolved. The priest further detailed several other instances in which he was involved with young adolescents sexually. In fact, he admitted to a life-long struggle with sexual impulse control and detailed his various attempts to get help.

Sure enough, the personnel files contained reports of repeated attempts by the priest himself to bring his sexual history to light. This priest had volunteered for psychiatric hospitalization on two previous occasions. Sadly, he was "treated" on both occasions for what was then viewed as "homosexual perversion." The first hospitalization occurred almost thirty years prior to the latest allegation. While there was certainly some talk of his sexual acting-out with adolescents during treatment, the ephebophilic nature of his attractions was seen then as secondary to the more fundamental issue, the need to change his sexual orientation.

By today's standards most professionals would view this latter issue as one hardly needing treatment in itself, and certainly in no way essentially connected to the quite distinct diagnosis of paraphilic psychosexual disorder that now seems to be this priest's primary diagnosis. In reviewing this case, it is sadly interesting to note that these "treatments" took place at one of the nation's leading psychiatric facilities. Few could have known thirty years ago what we now take for granted about the diagnosis and treatment of sexual anomalies or paraphilias [the generic term for sexual attractions or behavior that are considered unusual or "beyond" the norm]. As more and more came to light about this priest and his sexual behaviors, it also became clearer that he had attractions to and sexual behavior with even younger children (pre-pubescent), and that he had also told superiors about this activity and begged for help.

Hindsight is always clearer and cleaner. This minister, who is still regarded as one of the kindest and most helpful priests of his era, has himself lived through a hell. He is acutely aware of the hell he has created for so many others. He is deeply remorse-full and knows he can never trust himself with what he now recognizes as a permanent skew to his sexual life. He is finally receiving specific treatment for his disorder.

9. Hot-Tub Harry

This is the story of how what might look like innocent horseplay one moment can precipitate serious consequences only a few hours later.

Harry was a very successful pastor of a large suburban parish. He was known as a gregarious man, full of "fun" and a real party person, but also always eager to help any and all in the parish. He was generally be-loved by all. So it came as no surprise when he received his own invitation to join two of the local couples at their "Brand New Hot-Tub Christening." The new tub was outdoors off their new deck; the children had been farmed-out for the evening, and a good time was expected by all. After the barbecue and lots of celebratory cocktails, they all settled in to have fun. A few more drinks were provided on the edge of the tub and they were all "well oiled" by the time evening came.

It was at this point that Father, sipping yet another glass of wine, complained that all this material in his swimsuit was just "getting in the way." With that comment he immediately removed his swimsuit and threw it playfully across the tub. It struck one of the women in the side of her head. They all laughed anxiously at the time but seemed amused more than anything else.

Upon more sober reflection, the woman who had been hit with the swimsuit phoned the chancery early the next morning to complain of Father Harry's indecent behavior. In fact, she charged him with verbal sexual impropriety and sexual assault. (At least it was not alleged that it was assault with a deadly weapon, his swimsuit.)

As an initial investigation got started by religious authorities, more and more people spoke of Harry's "inappropriate" comments and of the discomfort they would feel around him sometimes. A litany of at least verbal insensitivities began to mount. As this incident got some exposure around the parish, other parishioners came forward and told of additional comments of a sexual nature that had

33

made them uncomfortable. Piece by piece, a rather bleak picture of gross immaturity, at best, emerged. In the worst case scenario, Harry was building a case against himself by being seen as guilty of repeated acts of sexual misconduct of a verbal nature, and a few where he made gestures of a compromising nature.

Harry's plug was pulled. After a thorough psychological assessment, it became more clear that Harry did, indeed, have some significant psychosexual issues that needed treatment. They were mostly in the area of repression and immaturity around sexual issues, but no one could rule out further trouble if Harry was left "in office" and without treatment. He was removed as pastor and sent into treatment immediately.

10. The In-House Scandals.

Rather than comment on a specific case here, I want to highlight any number of allegations that have recently come to light involving seminarians, young people testing their vocations, faculties of formation houses, and other "in-house" activities. It is sufficient to know that allegations of professional sexual misconduct are occurring with frightening regularity within religious institutions and communities themselves. Often the victims are students or seminarians, novices or scholastics, or persons considering formation programs. Only rarely do these get the light of serious press coverage, but they are a very real and serious piece of this whole puzzle.

Some persons charged with the formation of younger members of their groups are taking explicit sexual liberties or using the intimidation of their privileged positions of power to court sexual favors. Reports of everything from spanking to fellatio [oral-genital contact] have been reported. Persons have been reported and assessed for sexual misconduct scenarios including mutual masturbation, performing careful inspections of the genitalia, naked and indecent physical examinations, and voyeuristic verbal ex-

34

aminations. And all, believe it or not, under the guise of actually performing important or required formation tasks.

Persons in authority and working entirely within the walls of our own institutions have not been immune to charges of sexual misconduct themselves. Persons at the highest levels have been seriously accused; some have been convicted or have otherwise admitted their guilt. No one, it appears, is immune.

CHAPTER 4

COMMON THEMES

The illustrations in the preceding chapter were intended to be just that, illustrations. It is by no means an exhaustive list of the kinds of sexual misconduct ministers find themselves involved with. I do hope, nonetheless, that it has provided a flavor for our continuing discussion. There are usually many questions that begin to arise at this juncture, for example: Is there anything these men have in common? Is drug and alcohol abuse a contributing factor in all (most) cases? What about "normal" indiscretions? Simple mistakes? Is there any such thing today? What do I do if I suspect something in a colleague? In myself?

These are not all easy questions to answer. It is very important to remember that to answer some of these questions with anything like definitive conclusions, we will have to know much more about clergy sexual misconduct than we do at the moment. While it may seem that there have been many cases from which to extrapolate more generalized answers, in fact there is very little scientifically reliable data on which to base secure answers. We have really just begun to study the men (and women) involved in this kind of misconduct. Treatment centers for clergy and religious are just beginning to collect and analyze the information they do have. There is yet no central clearinghouse for this information, and there are some who are frankly afraid to look too hard.

As a result, I'm afraid, what we do get from so-called experts are mostly generalizations and their own impressions or those of colleagues. Whereas this is sometimes valuable (depending on the colleagues and their experience), it is no substitute for scientifically gathered and collated data. If church bodies spent one tenth of the amount of money on research as they do on assistance and compensation, it would take us far.

So, beware of the experts in analyzing clergy sexual misconduct. It may be a far cry to move from what we do know of incarcerated sex offenders to applying that information to ministers of the Gospel. Or then again, it may not be such a far cry. We just do not know at this point. I would offer the same caution concerning treatment for clerical sexual offenders. What works best, what does not, how "safe" are the after-care provisions when these persons are released from treatment? These are all issues that have only anecdotal and impressionistic answers at the moment. Be cautious when hearing definitive analyses.

But surely we can say something. There have been enough cases presented over the past few years, and there is some information already gathered at treatment facilities, to hazard some initial guesses. Yes, we can make some initial observations; unfortunately, even these shatter some previously held assumptions about clerical sexual misconduct.

The first thing that needs to be faced squarely is that there is not a great deal these men have in common in many of the clerical cases of misconduct. Just look at the illustrations in chapter three. Is there a common theme throughout those men's stories? Not really. Persons accused of sexual misconduct come from all types of ministries, are of all ages and educational backgrounds, are both heterosexual and homosexual (and perhaps most don't know which they are really), and have very different "methods of operating." No single picture emerges, for example, that of the sexual "deviant." Go back over the case illustrations yourself and try to pull out common themes. It is not easy.

But knowing these cases intimately, and having the advantage of the initial survey of residents at one of the largest treatment facilities for clergy and religious in North America to which I referred earlier (Loftus & Camargo, 1994), we can make some interesting observations. Unfortunately, the observations are also frightening in some cases.

We do know that many of these men experience a keen sense of isolation and loneliness in their lives. It is hard to define more precisely, but it is there in so many. This is not the isolation and loneliness of the grossly introverted misfit. In fact, many sexual offenders are among the most outgoing, even gregarious, extroverts one could meet; some of the child or adolescent predators use precisely these social skills to lure victims. But *in their hearts* they tell of a sharp feeling of isolation. There is something in the socialization process in these men that has gone off on slant. Many of them feel particularly inept in social situations and particularly with peers. They talk of feeling bereft of any real connectedness with others; they are, in this sense, loners. Remember, however, that the loneliness only rarely manifests itself in ways that are obvious to others watching them; they are most often pleasant and out-going in ministry, for example.

To continue this theme, we can now add some observations from the first large-scale study of over thirteen hundred clerics and religious men. Not only do most of the sexual offender population appear not unusual in their interpersonal relationships in ministry, they appear to be among the healthiest looking group in the entire sample. Yes, in comparing psychological test scores from men admitting sexual misconduct with the rest of the non-misconduct population, the former appear to be not particularly "pathological." They score higher on ego strength and lower on anxiety and all other psychological symptoms of maladaption and distress. These men appear to be among the most well adjusted men in the sample. They seem healthy. As an aside, this may account for why treatment is often difficult with this population. Often enough, they are not sure they have really done anything wrong; they don't feel, therefore, a lot of compunction for their deeds, and they are not feeling much pain themselves—at least not until a trial comes up or they are incarcerated.

In addition, when looking at the larger sample, alcohol and/or drug abuse is not seen as a precipitating factor in most cases of misconduct. Nor is there any history of serious alcohol/drug abuse (or even misuse) in the family situation from which these men come. Finally, there is also little evidence for any other psychiatric or psychological problem in their own lives, or in the lives of family members. There is no serious history of mental illness, period.

In analyzing some common demographic variables that might describe and perhaps predict future misconduct, our study, at least, also came up short; although there were some interesting preconceptions shattered. Most of the sexual offenders in our sample were diocesan priests, doing parish ministry in relatively large urban areas, over forty-nine years of age when first treated, with at least fifteen years of ministry behind them before offending, from middle class families with little history of instability (as noted) and were engaged in relatively frequent and random sexual misconduct (as defined by four or more instances and/or partners).

It seems that some of the more common early explanations of clerical misconduct will not hold up. Only rarely is the minister's misconduct a single event, while under the influence of alcohol, or because of significant psychopathology or distress at the time. Just having "one too many" and making a "terrible mistake" can happen; it is not, however, the norm. Nor does it seem from this sample that social isolation in a small, rural area is the norm. Most offenders worked in large urban areas.

One thing you may have noticed, however, that does seem to bind these men together is that only rarely is their misconduct a single incident. Even when looking at the case illustrations presented above, there are almost always other instances of at least "boundary violations" that can be determined. It appears to be almost never an isolated incident, especially when other verbal or behavioral transgressions are examined carefully. In many cases, there are also written records of previous suspicions; often there is a clear history of complaints in the internal forum if not the external one.

This "paper trail" of previous reports of misconduct poses one of the most dangerous challenges to religious authorities. It is here that most cases of liability take shape. The law presumes that reasonable precautions will be taken to ensure public safety. When there has been some previous knowledge of sexual misconduct, or even vaguely sexual complaints against a person that have previously come to the attention of legitimate superiors, the presumption is that those superiors will have taken action to prevent any further incident. Sometimes, when the complaints have been only vague or diffuse in the past, superiors will still be held accountable based on the fact that they "should have known" that so-and-so posed a danger. One can hardly blame dioceses and religious communities for taking legal counsel seriously these days. This is why some public policies on sexual misconduct fashioned by churches seem draconian to many ministers.

There are, to be sure, other scientific studies attempting to detail factors in clerical sexual misconduct. They include fascinating studies of a more biologic nature, such as comparisons of CAT scans of the brain, or hormonal levels in the blood. Some seem to hold promise for a whole new way of understanding sexuality and particularly sexual deviations (see Fierman, 1991; Langevin, 1994). But they, too, are in their infancy as research and will have to be "normed" for a specifically ministerial population. It could be a while yet before we really understand significant factors involved in these cases of misconduct. In the meantime, modesty and caution seem to be the best course.

CHAPTER 5

ESTABLISHING BOUNDARIES

Over the next few years one of the most common phrases heard in conversations among ministers will be that of "professional boundaries." This has become *the* description for the discussion of sexual ethics among all professionals in the nineties. There is much that has already been offered for professionals like physicians and lawyers, and a little bit that is beginning to come to the fore for religious professionals. There will be much more in coming months and years.

Again, the present treatment is intended to be an introduction only. I hope that we can shift the framework a bit from what has already become commonplace in religious conversation about boundaries and begin thinking about some important questions in regard to your own self-knowledge or lack thereof.

Two immediate cautions come to mind. The first is the realization that some ministers recoil at the very use of the word "professional." This is not how they see their roles within their communities; they are facilitators, or animators, or anything but "professional" in their pastoral concern. They do have a point. There is an interesting history here in the shift to the "professionalization of ministries." A recent, brief overview was provided by an article in the

Journal of Religion and Health (Vogelsang, 1994). Nonetheless, I would suggest that regardless of our own preferred description of ministry, we would do well to realize how our broader, secular culture does in fact view us. It is as "professionals." We will be viewed thus and regulated thus from this day forward. I do not believe there is any turning back on this clock. As said earlier, we are viewed as powerful men and women, and our relationships with those in our charge will always be seen as inequitous and based on inequity in power.

The second caution concerns the frightening narrowness with which some conversations about boundaries are already being shaped. Far too many ministers seem to think that the task before us is to draw-up lists of "rights and wrongs," do's and don'ts" to cover every conceivable situation we might encounter. "If we can only produce a handbook with clear and rigid guidelines," they deduce, then everybody will always know what they are doing. This is the same dynamic that got so many adolescent morality manuals in trouble. It is a markedly adolescent way of approaching the issue.

There is little doubt that such a "handbook of guidelines" for ministers will be produced in the not-too-distant future. Civil and criminal officers will demand one. And it is imperative that ministers themselves begin to engage this process and provide thoughtful input to the discussion. A "Code of Ethics" is, it seems to me, inevitable, and we ministers had better prepare our thoughts and feelings now. The National Federations of Priests' Councils in both the United States and Canada have begun such a process. They will need help. We will, after all, have to live with the consequences—all of us.

But a code of ethics is, or ought to be, the end product of a lot of serious soul-searching. And that search needs to begin with our own soul. The rest of this chapter will highlight some of the questions/issues to which we should be sensitive. They are offered for discussion and comment. Many of them are only starting points.

My Own Affective Life: A Starting Point

Any discussion of boundaries must begin with my own self-knowledge, not some external code of conduct. How well do I know myself as a sexual being? How well do I know, and how well can I appreciate, the place of sexuality in my ministry? Sexuality constitutes a very important part of all ministry. If nothing else, it provides the energy and dynamism to relate to others in their need. I am always a sexual person. My own energies, moods, and needs in this area have to be taken into account. They will be a force to be reckoned with whether I choose to be aware of them or not. We have learned over the past decades at least, often the hard way, that human persons ignore their sexual energies at their own peril. Sexual energy cannot be completely repressed while maintaining emotional or spiritual health. So, do I know myself and my needs in this regard? A series of pointed questions might be helpful. Questions do not have to be threatening. But they may be.

How have I (do I) handled sexuality in my life? Do I just prefer not to think about it until I have to? Is it only a question of "dealing with it" when I feel physically attracted to someone? Or titillated by someone or something? How have I grown (or not grown) as a sexual being throughout these years of my life? Am I grateful that I no longer "feel" sexual at all? Is it finally just about all over? What does that say to you?

What is my capacity for loneliness? People have different capacities, you know. Some feel the sometimes agonizing aloneness as a terrible burden; others carry it more lightly, almost as a gift. Most adults who have lived any length of time realize that everybody is lonely. Celibate ministers do not have this market cornered. There is, if you will pardon the philosophical slant, an existential separateness about all of us. Married couples of thirty years feel it as deeply as celibate monks. A minister told me recently of a married man who commented to him about loneliness this way: "You don't know what real loneliness is until you have just had a fight with your wife, are not speaking at the

45

moment, and it comes time for bed. You lie there with the woman you love so deeply and can't speak. You know that as close as you rest together, you are alone." That's loneliness.

Other terribly important questions about self-knowledge with regard to sexuality are focused around sexual orientation. Do I view myself as predominantly heterosexual or homosexual? How do I know? How do I think I know? Is it just because of some experiences I have had, or is it my fantasy life, or a combination of both? How do I feel about whatever answers I can give to the above questions? Does my sexual "map" disturb me? How so? How much? Is it something I would (could) share with another comfortably? Be honest now! Have I talked about this area of my life? With anyone other than a secret confessor? As far as I know, how do others view my sexual orientation? Do others think of me as homosexual? Heterosexual? Would anyone have the faintest idea? Or care?

What kind of sexual (genital) experience have I had, if any? How has that been integrated, if at all, into the rest of my life? Do I long for genital sexual experiences? How well do I know my fantasies, my desires, my dreams in this regard? Do I long for nothing? What has my sexual experience taught me about myself emotionally? Spiritually? Physically?

What have I learned about myself in my sexual exploration (or lack thereof)? What have I learned about others? How have I allowed (or not allowed) my sexuality to enter into my ministry? Do I consider sexuality an integral aspect of my personality? Do others? Friends, associates, parishioners?

These questions, and others like them, are not only healthy prods to general self-knowledge; they are crucial barometers in fashioning my personal "boundary." Without such knowledge of myself, chances are I will *never* be aware of transgressing my own or another's boundary. Here lies the real challenge for those wanting to minimize risk for sexual misconduct. I need to know me in order to know where my vulnerabilities expose me. It might not always be the same for others; they need to know themselves. Our "temptations," to borrow a moral frame of reference, will not be the same even in similar circumstances.

Clinicians who work with sexual offenders have long been impressed by the ability of such offenders to "compartmentalize" their lives. The same is remarkably true for clerical or ministerial offenders. Precisely part of the problem with these offenders is that they are able to block-out parts of their experience with remarkable ease. Whole aspects of personality suddenly "go silent." Values, commitments, convictions that are deeply and sincerely held cease to influence decision making. It is not uncommon to hear of a minister who works hard all morning at the parish in a sincere and well respected fashion, stops for lunch with the Ladies Home Guild, cheerfully performs several baptisms in the early afternoon, all the while receiving tons of genuine praise and gratitude. Then by mid-afternoon, he is cruising the local park for sexual adventure, has several anonymous encounters, and returns home just in time for evening benediction, where again he performs admirably. No one would ever suspect what Father does while they have afternoon tea. Even Father seems unaware.

Case after case of sexual misconduct among clergy has this same feel. Ministers are able to package their lives in almost hermetically sealed little boxes. Their sexuality is held so tightly that it seems to live a life of its own—quite literally at times. Therein lies the problem. It does take on a life "of its own" and remains inaccessible to everyone, including the minister him/herself. Sometimes the "seal" around sex is so tight that it allows people to be engaged in explicitly, blatant sexual activity without even "knowing" the activity to be sexual. Most clinicians working with sexual offenders have seen this over and over. The perpetrators of serious and obvious sexual abuses will sometimes seem shocked and insulted that anyone should have interpreted their behavior as sexual. Yet to an even casual observer, the acts might have been atrocious. This is sometimes referred to as the extraordinary ability to "deny" among these men. But it is clearly more than simple prevarication. In my experience, ministers seem to have an even more finely honed ability in such "blocking" tactics. So-called "spiritualization" is often used to bolster this dynamic as well.

Our ability to compartmentalize crucial areas of our psyche is in direct proportion to our degree of self-knowledge. This is especially true in areas of sexuality. It is imperative to know the starting point in my very personal sexual history so that I can know specific areas of vulnerability in setting boundaries in ministry.

Needs and Expectations Intruding in a Pastoral Situation

Knowing when my needs/expectations may intrude in a pastoral situation. This is a corollary to the kind of self-knowledge discussed above. I need to know myself well enough emotionally to be able to tell when my own personal needs or expectations are intruding in a pastoral situation. Some ministers like to think of themselves as "above all this kind of stuff." They think of themselves as purely disinterested heralds of the gospel; there is never anything of tainted self-interest in their hearts. They are fooling no one but themselves.

We all do what we do because we enjoy it. Ministers are no exception; we do what we do because it is satisfying to us emotionally, spiritually, and often enough even physically. Have you never felt that wonderful exhaustion after a job well done? We like this kind of work. This is perfectly natural and even wonderful. There are so many rewards to a life in ministry, on so many different levels.

The question here becomes at what point does a very thin line get crossed? At what point are *my needs* becoming the determining factor in the ministry? I keep doing late night counselling sessions because I have nothing else to do anyway. Or I forge deep bonds with some parishioners because I have no other friends. Or I enjoy having young people around all the time because I can be the clear leader; there are no challenges to my authority. Or I deliberately focus on sexual counselling because I have no other sexual outlets in my life.

When does that line get crossed? There is never a simple answer; we are all made with mixed motivation built-in. You can see why no "objective" code of ethics will satisfy all cases. You need to know yourself. If I know my sexual orientation as primarily homosexual, and am feeling terribly frustrated by this fact, and then "choose" to spend most of my evenings "counselling" young adult men in great detail about their masturbation habits, and do all the counselling up in my private bedroom suite, I am a significant accident waiting to happen. By the same token, ministers who know themselves to be heterosexual, and perhaps equally frustrated, might not want to spend their entire summer holiday coaching the young women's swimming team.

Please do not get the idea here that sexual orientation is the only or even the most important factor in potential misconduct; it is not. I use these as illustrations of one kind of self-knowledge that can be important. I must try to know my peculiar vulnerabilities in all situations and at all times. This is asking no less of ministers than we routinely expect of psychotherapists. The latter are supposed to know themselves well enough, usually through their own course of therapy, so that they avoid these pitfalls. Unfortunately, we know from recent surveys among psychologists and psychiatrists that there can be no guarantees with even the most rigorous training.

At the very least, ministers must be made more aware of the ambivalent feelings they may experience in many pastoral situations. We need to talk with each other about these scenarios, openly and honestly. We are not exempt from the common ambivalence inherent in all human motivation; we must come to know ourselves better and better.

The More Subtle Violations

As we have seen throughout our exploration of sexual misconduct, there can be some pretty subtle and unseen violations of another's boundaries that can have serious consequences. A minister does not need to charge into physical contact with another in order to violate him/her. One of the easiest illustrations is in the use of language. Giant companies, government agencies, whole professions have now recognized that language can create an atmosphere of violation that can be as serious as direct physical threats. Verbal harassment has become much more commonplace in our society. The United States government now speaks officially of "climates" of sexual harassment that are now specifically outlawed. We can easily become guilty of sexual misconduct because of the verbal insensitivity we betray.

Some ministers, unfortunately, are just becoming aware of this potential for harm in their pulpits and parish bulletins. Many find it difficult to distinguish clearly between simple "political incorrectness" and verbal assault; it is sometimes a judgment call. But remember that usually the person determining whether something is genuinely offensive will be the "victim" who felt it to be so.

There are also non-verbal ways for more subtle sexual misconduct to occur. What once might have been considered a simple gesture of friendship, such as a pat on the shoulder, or pat on the back, can now be taken as quite offensive. One needs to know a context extremely well before venturing to offer any physical gestures these days. A hug is sometimes *felt* as not just a hug. Common sense has to have a place here, but remember that common sense is not all that common. Modesty and caution are still good guides.

Although it hardly qualifies as a very subtle approach, physical massage needs to be singled out as a clearly ambivalent gesture. The exception, of course, might occur if you also happen to be a registered massage therapist. Most ministers are not. As the old saying goes, if I had a nickel for every case of sexual misconduct that started out as a "little massage for that tired back of yours," I'd be a wealthy man. The wonders that physical manipulation can effect need no endorsement from me; they are well documented in professional literature. But let professionals do it. Remember, what you *intended* to do will serve as a poor defense against charges of sexual misconduct. A very wise psychiatrist who worked with clergy for over thirty years and with whom I had the pleasure of working for many years used to say of priests being assessed for possible sexual misconduct, that as soon as he heard an opening line about an "innocent back rub," he knew he had "been there a thousand times before"; he could "smell it coming." He was almost always correct—and that goes back over thirty years. In the 1990s there is no such thing as an "innocent" back rub unless you are with your spouse or lover, or in a legitimate massage establishment.

The Need for Cultural Sensitivity

Some voice a legitimate concern that different cultural traditions have different norms and expectations in dealing with sexual issues, and even for physical contact between people. There can be no doubt that British tea parties bear little resemblance to Italian dinner parties. Cultural norms can be taken into account; language, gestures, and expectations do differ from one ethnic group to another. Here again, knowing yourself well enough to know the difference between a "normal" cultural expression of affection and taking advantage of someone (of whatever culture) is central. Just because in Zorba the Greek, men can dance with each other with arms and eyes locked in passionate affection, does not mean that the same will work in every ethnic Greek pool hall you discover at the edge of town. The motto for the 90s should be, when in doubt, think twice.

51

Knowing the Law

All ministers should have concise, specific, and detailed information about reporting laws in their jurisdictions. Some boundary violations, such as child sexual abuse, require immediate action in terms of reporting to local, civil authorities. I will not include details here for all fifty jurisdictions in the United States and twelve in Canada. But it is imperative that you know your own reporting legislation. In some jurisdictions, ministers *are* mandated reporters. In some others, ministers of the Gospel *are not* mandated reporters—unless they also hold another position, like school principal or guidance counsellor.

In almost all cases there is a "moral" obligation to report any seriously suspected child abuse under the law; there may or may not be specified penalties attached to non-compliance. All ministers should have ready and easy access to the phone numbers and/or addresses of appropriate child welfare agencies in their area and know the time limits for reporting when they are mandated reporters. In my judgment every religious jurisdiction (diocese, community) should have prepared a complete listing of this information for their membership and should forward it to each and every member. This information, which is often more important pastorally than legal norms, is often not included as part of a group's guidelines on sexual misconduct.

All ministers should also know their own church's guidelines on sexual misconduct and have ready the appropriate phone number and/or address for reporting to ecclesiastical authorities. There should be no delay in any case where you have serious reason to believe a child might be in danger. Contact civil and religious superiors immediately.

Avoid the Appearance of Impropriety

In today's climate there is a need for a conservative and evolving stance on sexual misconduct. Ministers must also recognize the need to avoid even the appearance of impropriety with all matters sexual. Sexual harassment, sexual exploitation, sexual assault, and sexual abuse are only a few of the relatively new descriptions of misconduct. As you should now know, some aspects of these behaviors are clear; much is still ambiguous and evolving. Anyone in a position of trust in today's society must recognize the potentially dangerous atmosphere in which we minister.

There will be much more discussion about the issue of professional boundaries for ministers. There will be workshops and literature becoming available. It behooves us all to pay attention and be part of the on-going establishment of appropriate guidelines. If we do not wish to be part of the solution, we will likely become part of the problem. Lamenting the course society is taking will, in the long-run, help no one. Ministers must attempt to become proactive. The place to start is with yourself. Self-knowledge is the key to any boundary discussion.

CHAPTER 6

CONCLUSION

At the risk of repeating myself and beating the proverbial dead horse again, let me offer a few random observations by way of conclusion. It should be clear that there is much that has not been said in the preceding pages. The intention was to spark conversation and discussion. If that has been successful, it may lead you to further exploration on your own, or with a group in which you feel comfortable discussing these matters. But do not think that all important issues have been handled. Fascinating and important concerns having to do with potential predisposing factors to sexual misconduct, diagnostic concerns, treatment issues, and deliberations about placement in ministry for the sexually abusive minister, stand out as only a few of the issues we have not even touched. Be careful of the "little knowledge" that can do great damage. At the same time, a few things ought to be clear by now.

The Problem Will Not Just Go Away

Despite some fervent wishes, it is imperative that we all realize that concerns about ministerial sexual misconduct will not simply disappear. This is not a momentary "blip on the radar screen" that will pass as soon as the press finds something else to worry about. As indicated earlier, although the problem of specifically *pedophilic* ministers may have run its course with media people for the time being, there will be new cases coming to light and they will spark just as much outrage and concern. Those with specific psychosexual disorders, like pedophilia or ephebophilia, do represent a significant portion of the ministerial population; almost 3 percent seem to show up in most surveys. Add to these the other larger pool of ministers who will compromise themselves in sexual ways with adults with whom they have a pastoral relationship, and you can see that this problem is not going to leave us for the foreseeable future. If you have your own fond wish that it will all just blow over, think again.

It Needs To Be Taken Seriously By All

All ministers need to take these concerns with deadly seriousness. This is not primarily in order to advance the old "C-Y-A" manoeuver (i.e., "cover your ass"), but because our *pastoral credibility* depends upon our being able to assume a leadership role within our communities around this issue. "Covering our own asses," in the sense of becoming more and more educated about sexuality and sexual misconduct for our own protection, is not a bad thing in itself. We need to be realistic, if nothing else. But there are more important issues at stake.

Our entire society in North America has become more and more sensitized to the ways in which we can sexually exploit each other. Our eyes and ears have become finely tuned to ferret-out abuses. We are learning more and more about just how prevalent these abuses are. For example, it is now commonplace to hear ordinary educated people musing about the prevalence of incest in our society; in fact, incest does represent, most likely, the largest percentage in terms of instances of child sexual abuse. We have become highly sensitive throughout the culture. Just listen to any talk show host on television or radio. Some have even suggested that we may be becoming obsessed with the whole topic.

Sexual misconduct should be addressed by leaders from every segment of our society—and that includes those of us who are ministers. We have a pastoral responsibility to become more aware at all levels and to speak out with courage and conviction about abuse. But many ministers are still "licking their own wounds" because of the allegations of misconduct among their own. They are afraid to talk about abuse or misconduct from their own pulpits. All our churches are paying a price for this reticence; we are no longer seen as credible spokespersons with the potential to lead. This is a real tragedy.

We need to take this issue seriously and continue to learn about all its various facets because of our pastoral responsibility, and as leaders in our churches.

The Need For Continuing Education

As a result of what was just said, all ministers of the Gospel and all who work with us need to have explicit and regular continuing education about professional sexual misconduct and all its corollaries. It is not enough to offer day-long workshops every three years (or as other litigation arises in the church). It is not enough to simply call in the so-called experts to pontificate periodically about theoretical issues of morality in contemporary culture. Many of these workshops have been well intentioned, no doubt; but they have also been widely experienced by participants as the old C-Y-A. Education about sexuality and sexual misconduct must be regular, focused, participatory, and required of all.

There is a special need to address the issue of initial formation for ministry. In many traditions (if not most) there is no regular course of study about sexuality. We still assume that these sensitive issues will "take care of themselves" somehow. Moral theology is still taught, of course, but with few concessions to the more mundane matters of sexual relating. Many ministers have still had no opportunity before ordination (and/or vows or call to ministry) to have had a single course in psychosexual development.

They will have had, no doubt, a weekend workshop, and that is supposed to suffice. Why our reticence? What are we afraid of? Is it our own embarrassment about sexuality? Or concerns about doctrinal purity? Are we *that* worried about the "thought police" of our congregations? Whatever its roots, it is exacting a high toll at this time in history.

What I find fascinating these days is that everyone seems to agree here about the need for initial and on-going education about sex. Just about every bishop or superior I have spoken to acknowledges the clear need—*in principle*. There's the problem. The conviction is in principle only. Don't let anyone actually try to introduce the course at the seminary! I have had personal experience now of two situations where just such dynamics were operative. In both cases the largest and most influential body of the church (bishops' conferences, etc.) made clear and specific recommendations to seminaries about adding courses of instruction about sexuality and sexual misconduct specifically. These were a matter of public record and, in fact, played well to the press and all the public. But in both cases, when the real live seminary faculty got prepared to actually change curricula, all of a sudden a "Doctrinal Board" of some sort appeared with enough questions and concerns to postpone the project for years. *In principle*, all were in agreement. In practice, nothing much has been done. This is a tragedy, and we will continue to pay a high price not only in credibility but in settlements and litigation.

We Are All Vulnerable

All ministers need to realize that in today's climate, we are all vulnerable. Very few of us are child molesters, very few are sexual predators, very few ever intend to harm anyone, but any of us could find ourselves involved in an allegation of sexual misconduct. The terrain has shifted. All professional relationships contain the seeds of disaster; we need not become paranoid, just sober and aware.

Ministers are particularly vulnerable, however, in two specific areas. The first has to do with vulnerability in

58

moments of "falling in love." I trust this "falling in love" is a wonderful dynamic that all will experience on several occasions throughout their lives. Falling in love is as important for celibate clergy as for married ministers. People can continue to honor their commitments and still find themselves head-over-heels in love again.

The second experience of particular vulnerability comes in just trying to express the affective dimension of our lives with our friends. Even ministers are just ordinary people; we all have emotional and affective and even bodily needs and desires. They are all good. Because society is peculiarly sensitive to ministers' boundaries these days does not mean that we should cease and desist from being and becoming loving human beings—with affective and physical desires. There is a real temptation with some ministers to throw the baby out with the bath water here. Yes, we do need to be more vigilant and cautious. No, we ought not jump back into a closet of totally repressed emotion and try to exist as windowless bumps.

An old man's sense of humor might help illustrate here. I had the honor of working with a community of brothers who had been devastated by allegations of sexual misconduct. In trying to just help them all discuss their feelings about the situation, a man in his seventies raised his hand. With a somewhat cynical tone to his voice, and a touch of mock anger, he said to me: "Frankly, I blame most of this whole thing on people like you, the god-damned psychologists. You are the ones who came in here years ago and told us all how out of touch we were with our own bodies, our sexuality, and all that crap! So we listened carefully, worked hard, and got more 'in touch'. Now look what's happened!" The audience roared with laughter, the kind of laughter that says: you know he's right. But you can't throw the baby out . . .

There is no turning back from the process of becoming a more loving and caring human being. Neither the experience of falling in love ourselves, nor the experience of just being affectionate and tender can be excised. We are human beings in the service of a gospel of acceptance and love.

We Are Powerful People

Let me simply repeat here what has been said several times elsewhere—because it is so important. Ministers are seen as powerful people in our society. Whether we *feel* powerful ourselves or not is not at question; we are powerful because of our roles and because of the heritage we represent. All our professional relationships are, by definition, inequitous. Whether you *intend* to hurt someone is never the interesting question; what the other person heard or felt or saw is what determines in the eyes of society what "actually occurred." Too many men are still saying "Oh, Pshaw" to this reality from behind prison bars. Forewarned is forearmed!

Guarding Against Paranoia and Depression

I feel very inadequate to the task here. All I can do is sound like an old-fashioned preacher and tell you what I think we must do. I can not tell you *how to do it*. But I know that there is a creeping paranoia becoming more and more palpable among clergy and ministers. If you have read this far, it is easy to understand why.

Ministers are getting so careful about guarding their affections that they are "shutting down" emotionally. Some are feeling more and more isolated. Some are becoming more afraid to even talk about their frustrations because someone is liable to feel the need to "report" their conversation—just to be on the safe side. If one is not careful, all affective communication can be curtailed out of fear. You become afraid to touch or hug anyone. You may even have heard stories of ministers being accused of impropriety at a ritual greeting of peace during a service. It has happened, frankly. Then there is the priest who told me recently that even at baptisms, he has stopped placing his hand on the baby's head lest someone misinterpret his intentions. Or the priests who will no longer counsel or hear the confessions of students unless in an open room with a clear-glass window and someone monitoring from outside. This is frightening stuff.

Then there is the temptation to extrapolate from ordinary living situations to the worst-case-scenarios in which you could conceivably be accused of misconduct. Fantasy can play dangerous tricks. I think of one long-time seminary professor who told me of his decision to abandon his teaching career because he no longer felt he could live with the students he taught without potentially compromising his integrity. To his mind, living with students created an *ipso facto* conflict of interest in today's climate. To be quite literal, you know, he probably is right. But how far can we allow common sense to be stretched?

The key to avoiding a crippling paranoia about sexual misconduct, it seems to me, lies in being able to be open and honest with myself and others about myself and my own affections. Again, it is a question of self-knowledge, and a kind of self-knowledge that can be shared with another whom you can trust. As in dealing with victims of abusive relationships, being able to "tell the secret" is critical. As ministers, we need to be able to start talking with each other about our feelings, perhaps especially our feelings of paranoia. We need to acknowledge our sexual feelings, our attractions, our desires, our longings, our "temptations." In darkness, paranoia thrives.

A final note here is equally important. Remember the old sage's line: just because you are paranoid, don't think they are not out to get you! These are dangerous times in which to be a minister. Be modest in your assessment of the dangers, and be cautious in how you behave.

I conclude with the line offered by Sergeant Phil Esterhouse on the old "Hill Street Blues" television show. At the beginning of each episode he would exhort his officers: "Be careful out there"!

We can do no less.

REFERENCES
AND RESOURCES

Berry, Jason. *Lead us not into temptation: Catholic priests and the sexual abuse of children.* New York: Doubleday, 1992.

> Written by a journalist who has become a familiar face to thousands of television viewers throughout the United States. Berry documents the scandal as it develops in the U.S. and the ineptitude of church officers in handling abuse situations. He mistakenly blames much of the problem on homosexuality issues, but offers a chilling commentary on the consequences of clerical abuse.

Burkett, Elinor and Bruni, Frank. *A gospel of shame: children, sexual abuse, and the catholic church.* New York: Viking, 1993.

> This is another journalistic description of the sex abuse crisis. It is more balanced and nuanced on the whole than Berry's, but tells much of the same bleak story. One of these two should be required reading for all ministers.

Fierman, Jay. (ed.) *Pedophilia: biosocial dimensions.* New York: Springer-Verlag, 1991.

> This is a collection of very sophisticated articles by some of the most respected researchers and theorists in the world. It advances a new way of looking at

psychosexual growth and its abberations; the book is difficult but rewarding reading for those interested in cutting-edge theory.

Irons, Richard. "The sexually exploitive professional: an addiction sensitive model for assessment." *Monograph of the second annual conference on addiction: prevention, recognition, treatment.* Behavioral Care Network & Abbot Northwestern Hospital, November, 1991.

Langevin, Ron. *Sexual strands: understanding and treating sexual anomalies in men.* Hillsdale, N.Y.: Lawrence Erblaum, 1983.

An early but comprehensive survey of research methodologies in assessing sexual anomalies from one of the significant researchers in the field.

Langevin, Ron. "Selected CAT scan studies in pedophilic men." *Annals of sex research.* Etobicoke, Ontario: Juniper Associates, 1994. (In press)

A very technical description of early promising studies of biologic differences in sexual offenders. This piece is mentioned in the text.

Loftus, John Allan, and Camargo, Robert, J. "Treating the clergy." *Annals of sex research.* Etiobicoke, Ontario: Juniper Associates, 1994. (In press)

This is a brief description of the Southdown treatment facility's twenty-five year retrospective study on a population of over thirteen hundred male residents. It summarizes the more technical information presented in other research publications.

Loftus, John Allan. *Sexual abuse in the church: a quest for understanding.* Aurora, Ontario: Southdown, 1989.

This brief pamphlet was one of the first to attempt to situate the clergy sexual abuse crisis in a context and ask some fundamental questions. It offers opinions that have been largely supported by subsequent research.

Manchester, William. *A world lit only by fire: the medieval mind and the renaissance: portrait of an age.* Boston: Little, Brown & Co., 1992.

> An extremely lucid and well written account of the church in the fifteenth and sixteenth centuries. It should provide consolation for any who think it could not possibly get any worse than it is today.

Money, John. *Love maps: clinical concepts of sexual/erotic health and pathology, paraphilia, and gender transposition in childhood, adolescence, and maturity.* New York: Prometheus Books & Irvington Press, 1988. (Paperback)

> This is a classic treatment of just about everything you've wanted to know about sexual development. Money is considered one of the most expert researchers and theorists in the field. It can be difficult going at times, but well worth it. There is also a bibliography that might be helpful. Also be aware that Money has several later volumes of similar interest.

Rosetti, Stephen (ed.). *Slayer of the soul: child sexual abuse and the Catholic church.* Mystic, CT: Twenty-third Publications, 1990.

> This is an excellent and very helpful collection of essays about child sexual abuse by clergy, written by many people with first-hand experience. It remains one of the earliest and most thoughtful commentaries available.

Saint Luke Institute. "A descriptive study of sexually abusing clergy." Suitland, MD: St. Luke Institute, 1993. (This is, as far as I know, still unpublished but should be available from St. Luke's directly.)

> A research study based on the St. Luke Institute population of clerical sexual offenders. This was a presentation at the Association for the Treatment of Sexual Abusers Conference in Boston, 1993.

Sipe, A.W. Richard. *A secret world: sexuality and the search for celibacy.* New York: Brunner/Mazel, 1990

Though not specifically on sexual misconduct, this provocative book offers an original interpretation of some classic understandings of celibacy. It also purports to be a result of some careful research by the author; in this regard it is less satisfying.

Vogelsang, John D. "Reconstructing the professional at the end of modernity." *Journal of religion and health,* Vol. 33, No. 1 (Spring, 1994) 61-72.

A rather dense piece at times and theoretical in the extreme. However, there is an interesting discussion on how ministry became associated wtih the "professions" in the course of recent history. Mentioned in the text.